Facts About the Alaskan Malamute

By Lisa Strattin

© 2019 Lisa Strattin

FREE BOOK

FREE FOR ALL SUBSCRIBERS

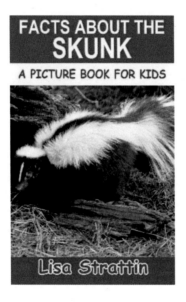

LisaStrattin.com/Subscribe-Here

BOX SET

- **FACTS ABOUT THE POISON DART FROGS**
- **FACTS ABOUT THE THREE TOED SLOTH**
- **FACTS ABOUT THE RED PANDA**
- **FACTS ABOUT THE SEAHORSE**
- **FACTS ABOUT THE PLATYPUS**
- **FACTS ABOUT THE REINDEER**
- **FACTS ABOUT THE PANTHER**
- **FACTS ABOUT THE SIBERIAN HUSKY**

LisaStrattin.com/BookBundle

Facts for Kids Picture Books by Lisa Strattin

Little Blue Penguin, Vol 92

Chipmunk, Vol 5

Frilled Lizard, Vol 39

Blue and Gold Macaw, Vol 13

Poison Dart Frogs, Vol 50

Blue Tarantula, Vol 115

African Elephants, Vol 8

Amur Leopard, Vol 89

Sabre Tooth Tiger, Vol 167

Baboon, Vol 174

Sign Up for New Release Emails Here

LisaStrattin.com/subscribe-here

COVER IMAGE

https://www.flickr.com/photos/ashotofwhiskey/9639196288

ADDITIONAL IMAGES

https://www.flickr.com/photos/untiedshoes_photos/5621777406/

https://www.flickr.com/photos/sirispjelkavik/456414625/

https://www.flickr.com/photos/sirispjelkavik/456414631/

https://www.flickr.com/photos/statefarm/8504657429/

https://www.flickr.com/photos/53887959@N07/4985404452/

https://www.flickr.com/photos/randihausken/407215321/

https://www.flickr.com/photos/omg-itzjazzi/3229023754/

https://www.flickr.com/photos/randihausken/431778417/

https://www.flickr.com/photos/tuxified/4912972823/

https://www.flickr.com/photos/jsf539/4650454504/

Contents

INTRODUCTION

The Alaskan Malamute was first bred as a working dog that could pull heavy loads in the very harsh winters. They were used by the Innuit people to pull heavy sleds and to help hunt seals for the peoples' survival.

Stormwinds Causin Chaos

BEHAVIOR

The Alaskan Malamute is a very intelligent dog and will be bored if there is not enough mental or physical exercise. They are affectional and loyal dogs that are totally devoted to their owner. They are known to exhibit traits of dominance over other breeds in a household.

APPEARANCE

The Alaskan Malamute looks a lot like a wolf, but they are not descended from the wolf at all. They have been bred from other domestic dog breeds. They have a strong body that is broad and heavy-boned. They are generally longer than they are tall with a double coat of fur that protects them from harsh cold temperatures. They are found in several colors, from black, gray or red, but all with the similar white markings in their fur. Their tail is naturally curved upwards.

BREEDING

The Alaskan Malamute is a working dog. Originally they were bred for helping people as they moved from Asia to the Arctic and back. They are able to handle very heavy loads and to endure very difficult winters.

LIFE SPAN

The Alaskan Malamute usually lives to about 14 years of age.

SIZE

The Alaskan Malamute adult dog grows to be about 2 feet tall and weighs about 85 pounds.

HABITAT

The Alaskan Malamute does well in regions with severe winters, although they are kept in some areas of the world as a pet that has more moderate temperatures. It is important to make sure that they are regularly groomed to help them to not suffer from too much heat due to their heavy coat, if you have one in a part of the world that has very hot summers.

DIET

There are many commercially available pet foods that are suitable for your pet Alaskan Malamute. As with any dog, if you notice a lot of scratching, there might be a food allergy to blame. Changing to another food can sometimes take care of this problem. However, if it persists, you should take your pet to a veterinarian to have them identify the specific issue that is causing this.

Good quality food and fresh water are the most important requirements for your pet.

INTERESTING FACTS

The Alaskan Malamute is usually not as fast as other breeds in long-distance sled racing, however, for the heavy workload, they just can't be outdone! They are affectionate, but not much good as a watchdog, in general. They are not as obedient as other dogs, so if you want a dog that does tricks on command, they might not be the right choice for you.

SUITABILITY AS PETS

These Alaskan Malamutes make excellent pets for many people. They don't "perform" like some other breeds, but they are very loyal to their owner and affectionate.

They are a good-sized dog though, and you should have plenty of room for them to get exercise. If you don't, you will have a very bored pet. Plenty of trips to the dog park and lots of exercise can make up for this lack of space.

COLOR ME

COLOR ME

COLOR ME

COLOR ME

COLOR ME

COLOR ME

COLOR ME

COLOR ME

COLOR ME

Please leave me a review here:

LisaStrattin.com/Review-Vol-339

For more Kindle Downloads Visit Lisa Strattin Author Page on Amazon Author Central

amazon.com/author/lisastrattin

To see upcoming titles, visit my website at LisaStrattin.com– most books available on Kindle!

LisaStrattin.com

FREE BOOK

FOR ALL SUBSCRIBERS – SIGN UP NOW

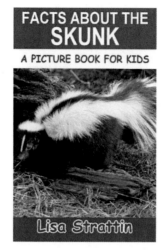

LisaStrattin.com/Subscribe-Here

LisaStrattin.com/Facebook

LisaStrattin.com/Youtube

Made in the USA
Las Vegas, NV
30 September 2022

56248774R00026